The Bug Man

Written by Zoë Clarke
Illustrated by Rory Walker

Collins

Max

Vik the Bug Man

Rav

2

bug van

Max and Rav jog the box full of bugs.

The box tips and the big bugs zip off.

Max and Rav mix socks and jam.

9

The bugs buzz into the jam socks.

10

Top six bugs

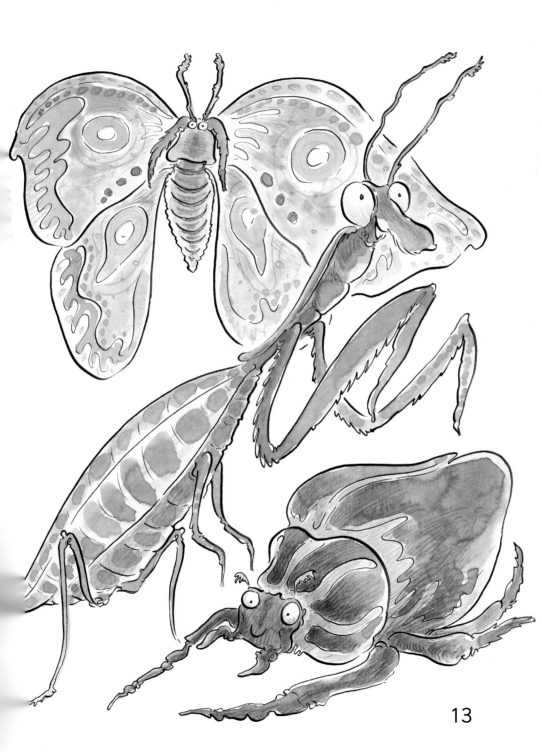

13

Map

🐾 Review: After reading 🐾

Use your assessment from hearing the children read to choose any GPCs, words or tricky words that need additional practice.

Read 1: Decoding

- On page 5, point to the word **jog**. Ask: What does "jog" mean? Encourage the children to read the sentence before deciding. Point out how it can mean run but here it means knock, nudge or push.
- Look at pages 4, 5 and 9. What words can the children find and read with the /v/ sound? (**Vik, Rav, van**)
  - o Repeat for the /x/ sound on pages 6 to 9. (**box, Max, mix, fix**)
- Model reading page 6 fluently and explain that you blended the words in your head silently. Turn to page 7 and ask the children to read the speech bubble. Say: Can you blend in your head when you read these words?

Read 2: Prosody

- Model reading page 6 expressively. Point out how this is a worrying bit of the story.
- Ask the children to read Max's words on page 7. Ask: How might she speak? How is she feeling? (e.g. *confident, rushed*)
- Challenge the children to read both pages expressively.

Read 3: Comprehension

- Focus on the topic of bugs. Ask: What bugs do you like, and why?
- Reread page 10. Ask: Why do you think the bugs buzzed into the jam socks? (e.g. *they liked the smell*; *they wanted to eat it*)
- Turn to pages 14 and 15, and ask the children to retell the story using the pictures as prompts. Ask questions to draw out the details:
  - o Who caused a problem? (e.g. *Max and Rav*)
  - o How did they solve the problem? (*they put a socks and jam mix on the van so the bugs came back*)
  - o When was everyone happy again? Why? (*at the end of the story because the Bug Man got his bugs back*)
- Bonus content: Turn to pages 2 and 3. Ask the children to think of another story about the Bug Man and his van. Prompt ideas by asking: Who causes a problem? What is the problem? Who solves it? How?
- Bonus content: Turn to pages 12 and 13 and ask the children to compare the bugs. Which is the most interesting? Why? Which can fly, jump or crawl?